Business ™
Transformed

Master the 17 Questions that Transform Business

By Paul Gossen
The Breakthrough Coach

Special thanks to Marilyn W. Atkinson Ph.D.
Powerful teacher, friend and breakthrough
thinker of The Art & Science of Coaching

LeadershipInc Press
Vancouver Canada V6B 2Y1
www.BusinessTransformed.com
www.17Questions.com

Library of Congress
Cataloging-in-Publications Data
Business Transformed, Master the 17
Questions that Transform Business /
Paul Gossen. 1. Management.
2. Business. 2. Leadership. 3.
Coaching. 4. Business transformation.

I. Paul Gossen II. Business Transformed

ISBN 13: 978-0-9783755-0-8
Printed in Canada.

Five Stages of Business Transformation

Relationship:
What if you were a master at building relationships, creating trust and supporting people to be their best?

Purpose:
What if you could cut right to the heart of the matter, powerfully define results and connect people with their energy and passion?

Transformation:
What if you could elevate the performance of your whole team in a single conversation? What if you could redefine what is possible, inspire people to act and to create breakthrough results?

Accountability:
Right now, as you are reading this, there are a number of promises that you have made and you have no real plan for how you will fulfill them. There are a number of people who have made promises to you, for which they have no real plans. This is a background source of worry and stress. What if you could hold them to account for and honor their intentions? What if you could assist them to be focused and productive in the face of anything? What if you were a master at creating strong agreements and supporting people to produce results at unprecedented levels?

Growth:
What if you could develop yourself and your team on an ongoing basis? What if you could create powerful insight in the face of any obstacle?

17 Questions

Contract	Can we talk?	1
Relationship	How are you?	2
Engagement	What do you want?	3
Purpose	Why is this important to you?	4
Accomplishment	How will you know when you have it?	5
Perception	What do you believe is possible?	6
Energy	What would be the breakthrough?	7
Performance	Who would you have to be?	8
Strategy	How could you produce this result?	9
Focus	How will you stay on track?	10
Reality	When will you do this?	11
Action	What if you don't do this?	12
Certainty	Is that a promise?	13
Accountability	Can I count on you?	14
Presence	Where was the breakdown?	15
Development	What did you learn?	16
Renewal	What's next?	17

Welcome to Business *Transformed*

As an executive coach, I witnessed time and time again the powerful transformative shift that would occur when my clients became clear on what they really wanted in their life and work. I also saw the powerful results they could produce when they had the accountability conversations required to put their plans into reality. This drew me to the field of organizational change where I was confronted by **the first paradox;**

Business cannot be changed.

Companies resist change. Organizational systems and procedures, by their nature, inhibit change. When I first began conducting organizational change programs I was astonished by how little impact they had. No amount of training alone would seem to stick.

Business can only be transformed.

I kept returning to the power of questions. I knew from my own experience that focused questions were the immutable force that powered business transformation. I also saw the power of questions everyday as I worked with highly accomplished business leaders. They seemed to have an almost magical ability to generate relationship and galvanize action in a short conversation. I could see that there were essential elements of this conversation that had to be completed in an exact order. For example, demanding accountability without first creating relationship would disrupt the intended outcome of the conversation.

I continued my quest to refine a simple structure for business transformation and began offering the questions to

4

managers, team leaders and executives to test. We became more structured in refining these essential elements and distilled the **17 Questions**™ that transform business. As the results came back, it became clear that **having powerful breakthrough conversations is a simple skill that anyone can learn quickly and easily.**

I began to get excited. What would a company look like if everyone had the ability to generate instant relationship, engage in breakthrough conversations and work with the highest level of accountability? What if we could distill these conversations down to their simplest form and put them into a package that anyone could use to produce results instantly? What if we could create a breakthrough virus that could rapidly transmit this capability to everyone in an organization? **The book you are holding in your hands is the virus.** You have already been infected.

Business Transformed is very simple. Read the book and start by asking "How are you?" The rest of the instructions are included. Let the questions do the work. Visit www.BusinessTransformed.com and download the free audio CD and listen to the 17 Questions. A relaxed and natural conversational tone is the key. Play with the questions and you cannot help but master them.

Business transformation can only take place inside of powerful questions.

 Paul Gossen
The Breakthrough Coach

What is Business Transformation?

Business transformation is a dramatic increase in the key performance measurements of a company or organization in a short period of time.

Business transformation is not radical. Most businesses have experienced some form of transformation in the last 10 years. Business transformation can come from ideas, technology, globalization, the Internet or new competitive business models. It is now well accepted that business transformation is a key element of the business cycle.

Most often business transformation seems random. Along comes a new idea, technology, strategy or set of market conditions. Yet some business leaders are able to generate business transformation on an ongoing basis, to transform business on demand.

This book offers a set of relationship, transformation and accountability questions that will consistently generate business transformation. **Some questions:**

How can we **drive** the process of business transformation?

How can we **accelerate** our rate of business transformation?

How can we **define** the competitive landscape? Lead rather than follow?

The power of questions

Almost every great business or management book offers ideas, stories, strategies or tips on how to be successful. More ideas, stories, strategies and tips, however educational and entertaining they may be, will not transform business. **What will transform business?**

The answer: **Great Questions.** Where did all those great ideas and strategies come from in the first place? Someone first asked a great question. If you want to become a great manager and leader, start asking great questions. If you want to lift the fog of *busy-ness* and increase the intelligence of your people, start asking great questions.

Something magical happens when a question is asked powerfully inside a committed conversation. In the 5 to 10 second **pregnant pause** after the question is asked, the real work happens.

Are you interested in a new level of relationship, transformation and accountability in your organization? **What will it take to stop being *smart* and start asking questions?**

Let the questions do the work. Transformation happens in the silence after a question.

Consider that you rarely give your full attention to anyone.

What else are you listening to instead?

Generally, you are listening to yourself.

There is a set of conversations that you have with yourself or others over and over again. These repeated conversations rarely produce results and usually leave you stuck in a position with a single point of view.

In order to use this book you will have to practice giving your full attention to the people with whom you are talking.

You will have limited success as a leader until you master the art of listening.

Listening principles

1 **Is your mouth moving?** If your mouth is moving you are not listening. Don't talk while listening.

2 **Let them finish:** Are they finishing sentences? 'Yes butting' and chewing the ends off other people's sentences is a sign you think that what you have to say is more important. It isn't. Get interested in them.

3 **Wait before speaking:** Ask yourself, "What did they just say?" then speak. Remember to **w.a.i.t.** = why am I talking?

4 **Ask, then wait:** A great question can take 60 seconds to process. Let them sort it out.

5 **Recap:** Start with "What I heard you say was..." and say exactly what they said back to them. What happens when you recap precisely? People experience that you understand them and they begin to go deeper into the conversation.

6 **Give up a judgment:** Is your judgment or story about someone so loud that you can't hear them? Give it up. Replace it with a new story such as "I am committed to doing what it takes to support them."

7 **Get comfortable with silence:** Silence builds the energy required for transformation. Let the silence build before speaking.

The question tree

There is no single formula to have a perfect business transformation conversation. Follow the guide and play with the questions.

How do I know which questions to ask?

Each of the 17 Master Questions fulfills a specific function. Within each question are a number of subquestions.

Don't ask all the subquestions at once. Pick a few and try them out. See which questions have the biggest impact. Start by asking them in order. As you practice **feel free to change the order.** Over time your intuition will guide you through the question tree.

After each question there are 3 main choices:

  1 **Recap and pause:** This says, "I heard you completely and I invite you to go deeper into your response."

  2 **Subquestion:** Ask an indented subquestion. This will take you further along the same line of questioning. You can also ask **"and what else?"** to go further on this line.

  3 **Next question:** Move to the next question or jump to the next of the 17 Master Questions.

Context: It is up to you to set the context and reformat the questions for personal life, work, team, customers or a global context. Start personal and build toward global.

Team: If you see this icon 🐾, we are talking to a team or group of people who work together.

How to ask the questions

The question flow:

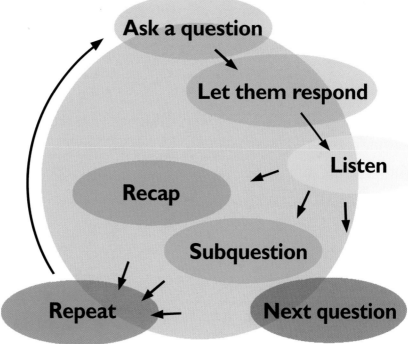

More guides:

The Unspoken Question: The Unspoken Question is at the heart of each of the 17 Questions. Don't ask the Unspoken Question. Allow it to become present.

Objections: Expect people to object. Objections are part of the conversation. Address the objection and gently guide them back into the question.

Exit: There are simple exit conditions that will let you know when to move to the next question.

How to approach this book:

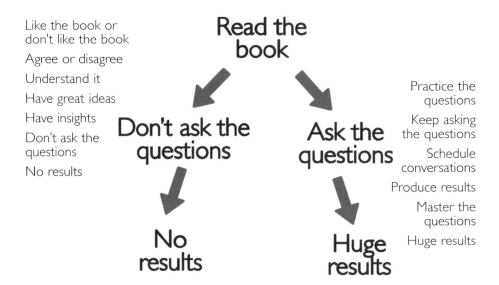

Like the book or don't like the book

Agree or disagree

Understand it

Have great ideas

Have insights

Don't ask the questions

No results

Read the book

Don't ask the questions

Ask the questions

Practice the questions

Keep asking the questions

Schedule conversations

Produce results

Master the questions

Huge results

No results

Huge results

Don't try to understand this book.
Just start asking the questions.

The book you are holding is like the tiny visible part of a huge iceberg. You can only see the rest of the iceberg by asking the questions. Before reading further, decide which path you will take.

5 Principles for asking the questions:

1. Let the questions do the work. Just ask the questions and get out of the way.
2. Make notes of the key ideas as they emerge.
3. Separate the questions. Go through them one at a time.
4. Recap: "What I heard you say was..."
5. Repeat and rephrase the questions. Keep asking "...and what else?"

The bad news is that business transformation cannot be explained. Talking about business transformation is not the same as experiencing business transformation. This book provides the model for business transformation. You are going to have to test it out and learn how to apply the questions and have powerful conversations. Are you up for the challenge? Begin with the following exercise. **Imagine:**

It is 90 days from today:
You read the book.
You asked the questions.
The questions worked.
You practiced the conversation.
What is your work and life like now that you have mastered **Business *Transformed?***

Business *Transformed* habits

Business *Transformed* is:

Asking questions

Listening

Creating trust

Building relationship

How do I build Business *Transformed* habits?

Interrupting (interrupting with a purpose)

Asking difficult accountability questions

Having kick-butt accountability conversations

Business *Transformed* is not:

Chit-chat

Giving advice

Telling people what to do

Interrupting (biting the tails off sentences)

Abusing the accountability questions

Gossip   (talking about someone without an intention to support them)

Complaining   (talking about a problem without an intention to find a solution)

can we talk?

1

Can we talk?

Setting an effective **contract** is the foundation of a powerful business transformation conversation.

Hey, can I have 5 minutes to talk about the project?

OK.

A contract can be very simple. As simple as **"Can we talk?" "Yes."**

The point is to get a yes before proceeding. While you might be able to force a conversation, you won't have an agreement. When they answer yes, it is the first of the many agreements required for business transformation.

Be prepared. Plan your
conversation in advance.

What will you talk about?

How long will it take?

What are the parameters
of the conversation?

If we spent the next 10 minutes to resolve this, would that be a good use of our time?

Do I have your permission?

Contracts *drive* results

Set the Frame: The contract is where you set the focus for the entire relationship. If you set a small focus, you produce small results. If you set a big focus, you produce big results. How big of a focus are you willing to set?

Is this a good time to talk?

Can we schedule a time?

Can I support you to produce this result?

From the future looking back:

We had a powerful conversation. What did we accomplish?

Unspoken Questions:

Do I have your permission to lead this conversation and to ask tough questions?

Are you willing to be honest and really tell me the truth?

Do we have enough trust to create a big game in this conversation?

Real leadership begins
by **designing a conversation**
to generate breakthrough results.

Advanced contracts

Team: Can I have 10 minutes to discuss this project?

Can we set up a meeting to resolve this issue?

Who would need to be there to resolve this issue?

Looking backward from the future:

We had a powerful meeting.

What did we accomplish?

What was discussed?

What was resolved?

Unspoken Question: Do I have permission to lead the team through a different kind of conversation?

Objection: NO, we don't want to talk about that.

Response: OK. This is an important issue. When *could* we discuss this?

Exit Conditions:

Is there an agreement?

Is there alignment?

Do I have your permission?

What makes a powerful meeting?

After months of negotiation to set up the meeting, I opened with, "It is 45 minutes from now. We had an outstanding meeting. What did we accomplish?" They looked at me like I was from another planet. The silence was intense.

Then one of the executives spoke. "We have analyzed your proposal and resolved all the details. We have a go forward initiative with dates and we have resolved the budget." **The magic was that 45 minutes later we had accomplished everything.**

▮Paul Gossen

2

how
are
you?

How important are relationships in business? How interested are you in producing results?

When you ask, "How are you?" people usually answer with "Fine." They think that is what you want them to say. You could ask the question in such a way that they would actually tell you the **truth** about how they are doing and what is really going on. Try it out.

If you ask them how they are doing and they tell you and you don't **listen**, the real conversation is over.

Get authentically curious about how people are doing and listen intently. They will tell you exactly what they need to be successful.

Business transformation leaders are masters of instantly generating and maintaining relationship.

I understand you.

How are you?

Are you well?

How is...
[What you already know
is important to this person]
...coming along?

Is there anything that could stand in our way
of working effectively together?

Is everything in place to have
this conversation?

Is our relationship in good shape?

Unspoken Questions:

Do you get that I am with you?

Do you get that I care
and understand?

Is this a long-term relationship?

Do we trust each other?

How **are**
you doing?

**The only way to earn trust is to actually
be curious about how they are doing.**

We *understand* each other.

⁜ Team:

How are we doing?

Are we a team?   Are we **in relationship?**

Are we all here? Is the team in good shape?

What is the health of our team?

What is the truth about the current operating state of our team?

Are we crazy-busy trying to get too much done?

Do we have any broken promises or missed deadlines?

Are any of our projects going sideways?

Is there anything that we have stepped over that might get in the way of everyone being able to fully participate in this conversation?

Are there any broken agreements that need to be addressed before we proceed?

Our *well-being* is important.

Is there a basic level of well-being?

What is our existing level of trust?

What will it take to establish the next level of trust?

Objection: I'm too busy. I don't have time to talk.

Response: I understand and given that we are considering taking on this important new project, would you be willing to let me check in on you from time to time to see that you are supported?

Exit: Are relationship and support present?

One of my technology CEOs was a master at tough accountability conversations. He had a strong protected technology, a brilliant team and was great at closing deals. However, he had a very limited capability to generate and maintain relationships. His brilliant engineers would work insane hours, produce amazing results, burn out and then leave. His deals would consistently fall through because his customers didn't experience trust. His business cycle was a series of growth initiatives hitting against a glass ceiling.

The assignment was simple. He started by asking "How are you?" and listening before every conversation. At first he felt false and pretentious. Over the next few months we had a number of conversations. He began to see that he couldn't win the game without his team winning first. He began to get **authentically curious** about how his people were actually doing. Today his company is a testament to the power of this question.

The reptilian, mammalian and visual brain

archipallium limbic stem neocortex

You are hardwired for three thinking styles.*

Your **reptilian brain** has developed over millions of years to protect you. It manages your body and habits, and takes over in flight-or-fight emergencies.

Your **mammalian brain** is the source of your communication and emotions. All language takes place in this area. Humans are mammals and most mammals live in groups. In a group, communication is critical for survival, as is sharing the emotions of the group's leader. When the alpha wolf is angry, the other wolves get angry. When the alpha wolf is scared, the other wolves get scared.

Your **visual brain** is unique to primates and gives you the ability to see things that aren't physically here. You cannot think of the future without using your visual brain. Anything created by humans is created with the visual brain. It is the source of creativity and brilliant ideas.

Negative Reptilian

In business today, most people are motivated by the negative reptilian brain or fear of negative consequences.

Think back to a time you procrastinated until the last minute and then produced amazing results in a short time. You already know that fear is a great way to get into action.

The Stick: Some fear is necessary to produce results. Organizations without consequences don't produce results.

The problem with using fear to motivate yourself or others is that it is easy to get stuck in the negative mammalian brain and to fall into the looping pattern of talking about what won't work.

Five steps to engage your staff in negative reptilian thinking:

Step 1

You're all fired!

**Steps 2-5
no longer neccesary**

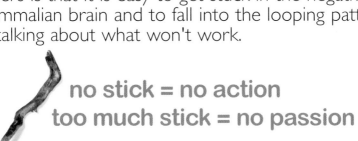

no stick = no action
too much stick = no passion

25

Negative Mammalian

Grrrrrrr, are you with me or against me?

Mammals love to communicate. Communication is how we assure our place in the group.

The problem is that communication without a clear contract to produce results takes the form of complaint or gossip. Complaint is talking about what doesn't work without a personal commitment to resolve it. Gossip is talking negatively about someone without a personal commitment to support them.

talk - contract = gossip

Complaint and gossip kill business transformation. Most people in business today are *dis*-engaged from life and work. We go through the motions and avoid pain. Being *dis*-engaged will not produce business transformation.

So, how do you *re*-engage in life and work?

By making a picture of the future you want.

The Visual Brain

The visual brain is unique to humans. Making internal pictures is a basic human function. You can't think of the future or the past without making a picture. You are already a master at using your visual brain.

When you are reacting to fear, you make pictures of how bad things could get and spend your time talking to yourself about how to avoid those scenarios. When you are doing this, most of your brain's power is being used to process fear.

What do I want for my life?

Making pictures of what you **don't** want is a great way to stop yourself from achieving your goals.

What happens when you make pictures of what you **do** want? What happens when you ask questions that engage your positive visual brain?

Questions *engage* the visual brain.

Paul Gossen

Positive Visual

It is no secret that making a picture of how you want things to go is a great way to improve performance. Top athletes have been using "visual rehearsal" for many years as a strategy to win gold medals.

Something amazing happens when you create a picture of what you want in the future. You engage the positive visual brain.

When you commit to a future that inspires you, something unique occurs. Your mammalian and reptilian brains are led by the positive visual brain.

When you create a picture of what you really want, you fully engage the unique capacity that is responsible for all of humanity's greatest achievements.

What will it look like when we all win?

To fully engage this capability ask:

What do you want?

what
do
you
want?³

What do you want?

What do you want right now?

> What do you want
> for your life?

What are your personal goals?

> What would make the
> difference for your... (pick one)

> > personal life?
> >
> > career?   team?
> >
> > company? customers?

If you achieved that, what else would you want?

> Where have you given up?

> What would you really love
> to have in that area?

Question 3 is a tough question to answer. Our day to day concerns are always in the way of seeing what we really want. It can take 1-3 weeks of staying with this question for it to 'pop.' After 3 weeks one of my clients, a successful restaurant owner, popped this question and realized that he wanted to be a successful independent filmmaker. He never took that path but rather went on to open a series of independent 'hit' restaurants. Eating in his restaurant was like being in a great film.

Clear Purpose

Would you be willing to consider that what you think you want is just the beginning of what you really want? Is it possible that you haven't even started to answer this question?

What gives you...

passion?   energy?

excitement?   joy?

If you knew you could produce the result, what would you really go for?

Logical levels:

We are always thinking on 3 levels. What do we want to **have, do** and **be**. Try the reverse order:

Who do you want to **BE?**

What do you want to **DO?**

What do you want to **HAVE?**

What do people say they want more than anything else?

3

84% of information workers say they want a 30% increase in salary. Take a moment and think about all the stuff you will buy with all that new money. Remember that within 90 days there will be a new thing you want more than anything else:

Another 30% increase in salary.

You spend so much energy wanting more money, that you have stopped asking for what you really want. **Stop that.**

If all your financial resources were handled for the rest of your life, what else would you want for your life?

What would you take on for yourself?

How would you spend your time?

How would you design your future?

What would you take on for other people?

Don't ask how yet.

If I knew I could produce the result, what would I ask for?

The default response when we think of a new idea is to ask, "How can I get it?" Consider that you have stopped asking for what you want because you couldn't see **how** to get it.

Don't ask **how** yet. Question 9, "How could you produce this result?" comes later. Asking **how** too soon gets in the way of your ability to consider what you really want.

For now, don't worry about how you are going to produce the result. Before you ask how, **get clear on what you really want.**

So, what do you really want?

Earn the right to ask tough questions

3

Why is knowing what you want in your personal life the foundation for business transformation?

This is a great question. CEOs and executives consistently ask me to present this work with the "personal life" questions removed. What they fear is that if they become too related with their staff, they will lose their ability to ask tough questions. In practice, the opposite is true.

Being related with your staff gives you the right to ask tough questions inside the bigger game of **supporting** them to get what they want out of their life *and* work.

The challenge is to **re-engage** throughout your entire life. Answer the "What do I want?" question for yourself, your career, your team and finally your business.

The job of business transformation leaders is to reconnect every *individual* vision for the future with a shared *organizational* vision for the future. Fortunately, this task is easy with the next question **"What do we want?"**

What do we want?

👥 **Team:**   What do we want for this project?

What do we want to accomplish as a team?

What would make the difference?

What is the key goal that will keep us on track?

What is the key target that we can rally around?

You will not find what you want by looking on your to-do list. Your to-do list will only give you more of what you already have.

What is our team *purpose?*

What do our customers want?

What do our customers want that they don't even know they want yet?

What do they say over and over again that they want?

If they had that, **what else** would they want?

What do they really want? What is the second or third level of what they want?

What do they need?

What is the need inside the need?

Unspoken Question: What is the bigger purpose that will provide a whole new level of engagement?

Objection: I don't know what I really want.

Response: Well, what if you did know, what might it be?

Exit: Was there a key shift in focus, energy and priorities?

Where have you stopped looking for what you want?

Most people spend life in a state of low-grade anger or frustration because they have stopped asking or are unwilling to really address the question, **"What do I want?"**

Where have we stopped looking for what we want?

Look into any organization and you will find that the vast majority of people have lost the connection between their work and what is important to them in life. **"What do we want?"**

The final question:

What does the world want?

Are you interested in unstoppable energy and momentum?

Are you interested in a breakthrough for your company?

Are you looking for a hit product that everyone wants?

Answer this question.

4

why is this important to you?

Why is this important to you?

Why do you want what you want?

Why do you like what you like?

You will only want what has **meaning** to you. You will only like what is important to you. That is how you are wired.

Meaning is your source of inspiration and action.

Asking this question will multiply your energy. With the right level of inspiration you can move mountains with tiny amounts of energy.

$E=MC^2$ Your Energy will always equal what is Meaningful to you, times the speed of light squared. (or a little meaning has a lot of energy)

Asking why is this important is *rocket fuel*

4

Why is this important to...

your life?

your family?

your relationships?

your career?

your work?

Really, why do you care?

Why else is this important to you?

What difference will this make in the world?

Unspoken Question:
What will provide a new level of purpose, energy and meaning?

4 Purpose

Why is this important to us?

Team:

Why is this important to... (pick one)

the team? the project?

the company? our customers?

Really, why do we care?

Why else is this important to our team?

What difference will this make in the world?

Objection: I don't really care. I only come to work because I have to. I have to do this or I will get fired.

Response: Even if you are just paying the bills, you are always working toward something. What are a few things that are important to you?

Exit: Is there a new connection to energy or enthusiasm?

Why is this important to the world?

4

What difference will this make in the world?

Why would someone in **Peru** care about this project?

What if it were 10 times more successful? What difference would it make then?

What would we need to bring to this project to make the most difference to the largest number of people?

For more **passion, energy** and **momentum,** include more people in the conversation

Positive Mammalian = Tone

Our speaking tone is how we communicate connection and emotion to the world. Voice tone can communicate anger, joy, urgency or relationship. Tone can communicate anything you want.

Tone is a key component of every powerful question.

Practice your ability to use different voice tones as you ask each question. Imagine that each question has a unique tone. Practice them all.

What would be the tone of... relationship?

action?

transformation?

accountability?

growth?

What is the tone of...

a powerful leader?

a wonderful teacher?

a business visionary?

how will you know when you have it?

5

Answering this question is the difference between quality of life and *endless* work.

"If we can't measure it,
it didn't happen."

Can you measure happiness?

Yes, you can measure happiness. Right now, think of ten ways to measure a breakthrough in your happiness. Which one would be the key measurement of your happiness?

Why would we even want to measure happiness? Something powerful happens when you put a key measurement in place.

You make the abstract real.

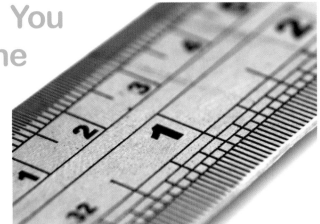

How will you know when you have it?

5

What are the specific results, in detail, that will let you know that you have achieved this?

How will you know when to stop working on it?

How can you make that specific and measurable?

What would the numbers be?

How else will you know when you have achieved this result?

Visual Test: What will it look like when you succeed? Where will the victory celebration be held? What color of shirt will you be wearing?

Unspoken Question: Have you actually done the work to build a specific future?

A measurement is only a measurement if there is a *number* involved.

5 Accomplishment

How will we know when we have succeeded?

Team:

How will **we** know when **we** have achieved this result?

> What are the specific results, in detail, that will let everyone know **we** have achieved this?

> What are the specific and measurable details?

What are the key numbers and metrics of **our** success?

How else will we know when **we** achieve these results?

> **Visual Test:** The CEO calls you into his office to congratulate you on the results. Wow. Do you ever feel great! You notice a beautiful flower on the CEO's desk. What color is that flower?

Scaling Questions:

Sometimes we draw a blank when we try to measure abstract concepts, such as happiness. A Scaling Question is a great way to keep the conversation flowing:

> On a scale of 1 to 10...   How satisfied are you?

> How committed are you to the success of the project?

What would you need to do to raise that by 2 points?

6

what do you believe is possible?

6 Perception

What do you believe is possible?

Can you predict the future? You think you can.

You are addicted to trying to predict the future. You spend vast amounts of energy trying to anticipate what is going to happen next. You are hard-wired to make assumptions about how it is going to go and repeatedly run scenarios of how you might respond.

This pattern of **reducing the risk** puts a cap on your ability to produce results. While it takes a great deal of your brain power to run these simulations, the real cost is much more subtle. **Your habit of attempting to predict the future displaces your ability to see the future you want.** Your predicted future, as you imagine it playing out, is riddled with assumptions about how you think it should go. Each assumption places a limit on what you could create. Each of these assumptions, when brought to light, is a perfect opportunity to create breakthrough results.

Can you predict the future?
No, you cannot predict the future.

Would you be willing to relax a bit and **play** with the future?

What do you believe is possible?

Would you be willing to question what is possible here?

If this project went really well, how well could it go?

Would you be willing to have it be...   (pick one)

   easy?   fun?

   successful?   under budget?   ahead of schedule?

If you knew it could go that way, would you choose it to go that way?

   What would that look like?

      Would you be willing to develop a plan for it to go that way?

      Would you be willing to work out all the details of that scenario?

   If you could have **it all,** what would **it all** be?

      Would you be willing to have it all?

         Could life be that good?

If you could only have what you *believe* is possible, what would you be *willing* to *believe* is possible?

What do we believe is possible?

Team: How do we want this project to go?

Because the project hasn't happened yet, almost anything could happen. Given this range of possibilities, what would we choose for this project?

> If everything went according to plan, what could be possible?

> What would we need to have in place for this project to be effective, well managed, finished ahead of schedule and under budget?

Objection: I already know how it will go because the last project went that way.

Response: How do you know that? This project hasn't even started.

Exit: Is there a space for new possibilities?

Would you be **willing** to upgrade what you believe is possible for this project?

Could it be easy?

Here is a powerful series of questions to move from no possibility to near certainty.

The sequence is:
willing   choose   plan   schedule

6

> Would you be **willing** to have this project be easier than you expect and ahead of schedule? **Yes**

>> If you knew it could go that way would you **choose** it to go that way? **Yes.**

>> What could that look like? Would you be willing to develop a **plan** right now for it to go that way? **Yes.**

>> Can we work out all the details and **schedule** this scenario? **OK.**

Unspoken Question: Would you be willing to consider that your results are limited by your expectations and that you are capable of much more than you think?

Test: Does this now seem achievable?

Visual Test: What will it look like when it is complete?

The Breakthrough Circle

Questions 3 to 8 form a conversational circle that can shift almost any seemingly insurmountable problem.

Stay in this loop until you sense a shift. People will always let you know when they are ready to move on in the conversation.

Input →

3
What do
you want?

8↗
Who would
you have to be?

→**4**
Why is this
important to you?

↑**7**
What would be
the breakthrough?

5↓
How will you know
when you have it?

6
What do you
believe is possible?

✔ Test
Has there been a shift
in energy or enthusiasm?

↘ Exit

"I read the first half of the book over the weekend and put the questions to use on Monday. In our first meeting, we looped through questions 3 to 8 and laid the groundwork for a powerful new management plan."

**Gord Murray, Regional Manager,
Golder Associates**

what would be the breakthrough?

What would be the breakthrough?

What is a breakthrough? A breakthrough is a sudden shift that takes our ability to produce results to a whole new level.

The only game worth playing is a breakthrough game.

A breakthrough is always available and waiting just outside our range of vision. What is the best way to see it? Stand in the future in which the breakthrough has already happened, then look back at *now* and see what happened.

What would it look like to have a breakthrough in the quality of your... (pick one)

work?   life?   health?

relationships?   career?

What would it take for you to produce this result easily?

What would be the KEY breakthrough that would make all the difference?

Stand in the future looking back.

It is 90 days from today. The project was highly successful. Looking back, you realize it was much easier than you expected it to be.

7

What happened?

What made the **biggest** difference?

Visual Test: What did the breakthrough look like?

What makes a breakthrough happen?
Asking for it.

7 Energy

⚞⚟ Team:

> It is 6 months from now.
> The project was a huge success.
> What was the key breakthrough
> that made the difference?

What would take this project to an entirely new level?

What would it look like to have a breakthrough in the quality of our...   (pick one)

> teamwork?   products?

> support?   communications?

If we exceeded our target by 20%, 50% or 100%, would that be a breakthrough?

If we achieved twice our current measures of success, would that be a breakthrough?

Unspoken Question: Would you be willing to consider that you could be playing at a whole new level?

Objection: I'm not sure what the breakthrough could be.

Response: What are 3 small things that might make a difference?

Exit: Is the breakthrough *calling* you?
Are fear or excitement present?
Is the team inspired?

who
would
you have
to be?

8

Who would you have to *be* to produce this result?

> Who would I have to be to create a breakthrough in this project?

Think about this:

You have no idea what your capabilities are.

We are not talking about unused brain power or some other possible concept.

Right now, with the right structure of relationship, support, inquiry, promises, confidence, accountability and team communication, you could be producing results at an extraordinary level.

We think we know who we are and what we can produce and thus we are trapped.

Who would you have to be?

It is 90 days from today and congratulations! The project is a huge success!

What kind of person did you have to be to produce this result?

Having completed this, what is your new level of...

commitment   focus

communications   energy

Visual Test: What does it look like now that it has been completed?

At what new level did you have to play to produce this result?

8

What kind of support did you need?

What new level of promises and **accountability** did you have to establish to produce this?

What new level of confidence did you have to develop to generate this?

What kind of communication had to take place for you to stay on track?

The role of a great leader is to ask the questions that allow people to step into their power and produce unprecedented results.

8 Performance

 **Team:**

What kind of team would we have to become in order to produce this result?

At what new level would we have to be playing?

What new level of communication would we need?

What new level of accountability would we need?

Unspoken Question: Would you be willing to entertain the possibility that we already have everything we need to be successful?

Objection: I already have too much on my plate.

Response: This isn't about more things on your to-do list. It's about the question of who you would have to be to take on this new project and still have more free time.

Objection: Why are you singling me out? You know I'm a team player.

Response: This project will require everyone on the team to be committed and function at a whole new level.

Exit: Is the team open to a new level of performance?

Seal up the breakthrough

Name it.

Names have power. When you give something a name you create a word that encapsulates all of the conversations you have had about it. Even if you have not yet committed to a project or process, the act of naming it gives it a life of its own.

Before we move on, would you be willing to name this project?

What would be a great name?

How else can you represent this project?

If the project had a color, what color would it be?

If the project were an animal, which animal would it be?

If the project had an icon, symbol or logo, what would it be?

Visual Test: Before we move on, take a moment and picture yourself having completed this.

What is it like now that you have achieved this?

When you picture it, what does your picture look like?

What is the color, shape, size and/or movement of your picture?

8

Welcome to the accountability section.

I am consistently shocked by the degree to which real accountability conversations are missing in business today. People talk about accountability, but usually they mean "Who will we blame, after the fact, when things go wrong?"

Managers, business people and especially project managers are very good at asking and answering Question 9, "How could you produce this result?" Unfortunately, after Question 9, the ability to resolve the rest of the accountability conversation often disappears.

The reality is that the balance of the accountability conversation is **displaced** by our body of unproductive habits, the flood of interruptions, our weak relationship with time and the fragmented way we make promises.

Accountability is actually a simple conversation that can be mastered by anyone with a bit of practice. Let's start a new conversation for a new level of accountability in business.

This new conversation begins with:

Our current level of accountability is *no* ⟵ *longer acceptable.*

> **Exercise:**
> Once a day for the next week, find an appropriate place to say this.

9

how
could
you
produce
this
result?

Real intelligence is the ability to engage in inquiry.

What are some of the ways you could produce this result?

> What could the plan be?

> What amounts of time, energy or resources would be required?

> What are the steps, stages and milestones?

> What would you need from other people?

What are some other ways we could accomplish this?

> Would you be willing to keep coming up with other possible ideas?

> > How else?

> > And how else?

What are 3 **other** ways we could achieve this result?

Break your addiction to strategy.

Coming up with the "brilliant idea" is not the point. The purpose of asking this question is to fully engage your team in the question.

Don't stop until there are many possible solutions.

Good, bad or ugly, write them all down.

Sort them out later.

Open Loop Questions:

Many people are not used to open loop questions.

That is, questions for which there are no simple answers.

That is, questions for which finding the answer is not the point.

Start slowly and develop your team's capability to grapple with open loop questions.

Whiteboard Exercise:

1 Outline the problem as an opportunity.

2 Number a large empty whiteboard from 1 to 20.

3 Come up with 20 possible solutions.

Last time I tried this I was working with a reluctant team. It took 15 minutes just to get going. After 45 minutes they had so much energy and momentum they couldn't stop coming up with ideas. On the whiteboard were 43 possible solutions to their problem.

9

What is team thinking?

 Team:

How can we include everyone in the project planning process, so that we all experience ownership of the ideas?

What are some of the ways that we could produce this result?

What are the key elements of the plan?

What is the project management process?

What is required in terms of timeline, resources, people, approval and budget?

How much of our focus will this take?

What do we need from other people?

Objection: What about all the failed initiatives and projects that didn't happen?

Response: Given that we have not yet promised to take this on and we can't even make a promise without addressing the reality of our available time and resources, would you be willing to explore some of the ways we could produce this result anyway?

Exit: Is there a list of 20 or more ideas that everyone has had an experience of co-developing.

9

What is the difference between my idea and our idea?

Why is the next section so long?

If we followed you around with a video camera for 24 hours and recorded all of your actions, it would reveal the truth about how you use your time to produce results.

If we tracked all the great ideas and projects you and your team have had or started, it would reveal the truth about your ability to stay focused.

How will **you** stay focused and keep this project on track?

How will **we** keep the **team** focused and keep this project on track?

how will you stay on track?

10

How will you stay on track?
or...   How could you stop yourself?

What might take you off track?

How have you stopped yourself in the past?

What could get in the way of your successful completion of this project?

What structures will you need to put in place to stay on track?

Who could you trust to support you to keep you on purpose?

CAUTION

RADIATION

Reptilian Mind: 'Habit without thought.' We love to immerse ourselves in repetitive tasks and mindless busywork. Why engage in those difficult conversations that drive a business forward when we can look through the minute details, endlessly check our email and talk *about* the problem?

The reptilian brain cannot transform business.

Tell the truth about your time.

You will have no power in this conversation unless you begin by telling the truth about how you use your time.

How do you use your time?

What are your work habits?

Team:

How do we use our time?

What are some common time-wasting activities?

How will we manage competing priorities, other projects and any other concerns in order to stay on track and be successful with this project?

92% of your time is spent on things that have NOTHING to do with what you want.

"Too busy doing what?"

 Team:

Given that it is easier to get lost in the details of a project than have the tough conversations that hold people to account, how will we stay on track?

How will we hold each other to our purpose in the face of our unproductive habits?

What structure will we need to put in place?

What are 3 simple ways we can stay on track?

Mastering your focus will allow you to produce unprecedented results with tiny amounts of time, energy and effort.

What are you doing *instead* of producing breakthrough results?

What activities are displacing the challenging conversations that will drive your business forward?

What are your negative work habits?

How are you stopping yourself?

What are one or two small things you could do to increase your effectiveness in that area?

Would you be willing to take on being strong in that area for the next week?

10

Adrenaline Addiction: There is a drug involved and that drug is adrenaline. Nothing gets things moving like a good emergency. Managers love to use adrenaline to produce results. We love the drama and excitement and the surge of *juice.* But there is a cost - your intelligence and your health.

Adrenaline will not transform business.

CAUTION

One Mind = One Activity

One of the great myths of the 1980s was that a person could do more than one thing at a time and would somehow be more efficient by doing so. Since then, study after study has demonstrated that the habits of multitasking reduce productivity by up to 30%.

Now that we are fully into the 'age of attention deficit disorder', how will you push back against the flood of distractions in order to produce high-level results?

Do one and only one thing at a time. If you interrupt yourself with a great idea, write it down and come back to it later. If someone else interrupts you with something that you could handle later, stop and schedule a time to give it your full attention.

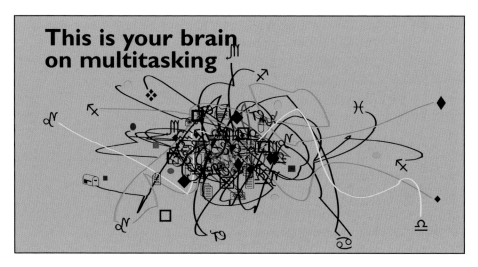

This is your brain on multitasking

Interruptions

Are you **weak** or **strong** with interruptions?

Are you the Receptionist?

Being the receptionist is a great job. The phone rings, you pick it up. Someone walks into your office, you stop what you are doing and take care of them. Simple.

Although helpful, the receptionist has a limited ability to produce high-level results. Constant interruption reduces your ability to think clearly. Are you being the receptionist when you shouldn't be? Are you being responsive instead of keeping your promises?

Are you the Fireman?

The fireman is a hero. You wait for the bell to ring, rush to the scene and put out the fire.

10

Putting out fires is important, but on its own will not generate a breakthrough in business. Constant emergency leaves you unable to plan your future. Are you putting out fires instead of keeping your promises?

**Functioning IQ drops
10 points when distracted by
ringing phones, endless email
and constant interruptions. This is
DOUBLE the 4 point drop seen
from smoking marijuana.**

2006 Study
Hewlett Packard,
University of London

Interruptions survival kit

Take control of your day.

1 Tell the truth: Do you have a weak or strong relationship with interruptions?

> How many hours per day do you spend dealing with interruptions?
>
> What are the main sources of interruption and distractions? (people or activities)
>
> What are the patterns? (times or business cycles)
>
> What percentage of your unplanned activities could be scheduled?

2 Cost: What is the cost of constant interruptions on your... (pick one)

> focus?   peace of mind?   life balance?
>
> reputation?   professionalism?

3 Schedule Everything: Don't just schedule appointments. Map all of your main activities into your schedule. The more you schedule yourself, the more you have to negotiate with and push back against.

4 Schedule Interruptions: How much of your day is governed by interruptions or unplanned activities? When do they typically come? Put several blocks of time into your day to deal with unplanned activities. This will also prevent you from over scheduling yourself.

5 Gaps: Leave gaps in your schedule. Scheduling your day with back-to-back activities is the perfect way to sabotage yourself. Always leave open buffer times between events.

6 Push Back: What percentage of your interruptions are real 'drop everything and do it now' circumstances and what percentage could be dealt with in the next 24 hours?

> Can we set up a time so that I can give you my full attention on this matter?

7 Close your door: Set up open door and closed door times with your co-workers (even if you don't have a door).

8 Stop interrupting yourself: Notice your personal interruption patterns, breaks, checking email and chit-chat. Make a pact with a buddy to be interruption-free.

9 Develop interruption agreements: Try asking:

10

"Instead of handling this right now, can we set up a recurring time to go through all the details?"

"Can we define what constitutes an emergency? If it isn't an emergency, can we deal with this in our next scheduled meeting or open door time?"

How many times per day do you check your email?

The average wired worker checks for new email 23 times a day, *debilitating* their productivity.

Email Addiction

Email is a great way to stay busy. If you check your email more than 5 times a day, you are addicted to email. The problem with constantly checking your email is that you train people that you are instantly available via email. Then you **have to check your email constantly** in order to be responsive. At least you appear responsive. Constantly checking your email has nothing to do with keeping your promises.

Email has replaced Starbucks as the number one white-collar addiction.

Email is not a conversation

Email has become the default communications channel of the 21st century. It is a quick way to transmit lots of information to many people. Email solves the voicemail trap.

However, email cannot transmit a speaking tone. Tone is the window to the mammalian brain. Tone is how humans communicate their emotions. A powerful conversation always has an emotional element. You cannot create relationship or have real accountability conversations without tone. As you read or write text, you imagine or assume an emotional tone. From email arguments to billion dollar cost overruns to real wars, assuming the emotional state of the other party is **always** the primary source of conflict.

Email is a great way to avoid having real conversations. If you spend more than 2 hours a day dealing with email, you are attempting to substitute email for real conversations.

10

Writing is slow. Explaining your point of view or justifying a decision via email requires you to compose text. Wanting to appear professional requires that the text be well edited.

**Stop wasting time.
Use email to schedule
real conversations.**

Telephone communication has 4 times the success rate of email communication.

Psychology Today, 2007 Study

The email rehab program

1 **Tell the truth:** What are your email patterns? How much time do you spend per day in email land?

2 **Response time:** Negotiate realistic email response times with your team.

3 **Email agreements:** Set up agreements not to use email for urgent communications and for matters best discussed in person or on the phone.

4 **Build your system:** Spend a little time to save a lot of time. Get beyond the 'send' and 'delete' email command. Your email program is equipped with easy-to-use features for filtering, searching, archiving, creating invitations and managing project and people folders. Design your system to serve you and *PLAY* with it until you have control.

5 **Action required:** Immediately separate **'for your info'** from your **'action required'** email. Deal with your 'for your info' email all at once at a later time.

6 **Time block email:** Schedule two or three 15-45 minute times to check email and respond to simple requests.

7 **Think before responding:** For anything that can't be completed in your set email time, estimate how long it will take and see where it will fit in your schedule.

10

8 **Stay strong:** Only check your email during your email time. If you need to check something, check your schedule. Next time you have a big project, try unplugging your email and see how much more focused you become.

9 **Pick up the phone:** Email is the perfect tool to schedule powerful **17 Questions** conversations.

10 Use email - don't let email use you.

After working with hundreds of managers, I am *shocked* by the degree to which the following question is missing in business today...

Busy Busy Busy

Busy ≠ Successful

Busy does not equal successful or important.

Being busy is a symptom of producing results at a low level.

Being too busy to think is a sign of disorganization and poor planning skills.

You are not paid to be busy. You are paid to produce results.

11

when
will
you do
this?

When will you do this?

Why do projects fail? Why are targets missed? Why don't good people keep their promises? The single reason is that people are weak at answering the "when" question.

If your promise doesn't have a solid plan with a realistic amount of time in your schedule, your promise is a fantasy. **Making a promise without a *realistic plan* is lying.**

What's your relationship with reality?

Most of your current promises have little or no reality. That is to say, you have no idea how and **when** you will handle them. Likewise, most of the people who make promises to you have no idea **when** they will do what they need to do to keep them. Unfortunately, you can't blame them because you accepted their promises as real, even when you knew they were not.

Is this project sufficiently engaging and meaningful that fitting it into your schedule will be easy?

When will you do this?

How long do you estimate that will take?

Is that a realistic amount of time?

Are you being overly optimistic?

How will you manage your time in order to be successful?

Do you have enough available time in your schedule to complete this on time?

Would you be willing to set dates for the key milestones?

Would you be willing to schedule those actions now?

Do you use your schedule actively?

What are your scheduling habits?

Can you trust your schedule?

Would you be willing to map this into your schedule as a series of times blocks?

Can you do that now?

Can you do that in the next 24 hours?

Can I count on you to manage your time such that **no circumstances** get in the way of you completing this project successfully?

Unspoken Question: Can I trust you to think through all the details and build a realistic timeline?

11 Reality

Team:

How can we manage our time and accountability at the level required for this project to succeed?

How will we have to manage our schedules so that we are successful?

Can we sit down and go through **our** schedules together?

Can we estimate how much time this will take to complete?

Is that a realistic amount of time?

Are we being overly optimistic?

Do we currently have enough free time to complete this on time?

Can we schedule this right now?

Are we willing to set dates for the key milestones?

Is this a deadline or a time block?

How do our individual schedules mesh with the team's schedule and timeline?

How will actions be tracked to ensure success?

Is the full reality of this project represented in our schedules and plan?

Can we count on each other to manage our time such that no circumstances get in the way of producing this result?

Business Transformed

When will you do this?

Objection: I don't know how long it will take.

Response: Would you be willing to make a best guess, pencil it in and track how long it actually takes? Would you consider that with a bit of practice you could be very accurate at estimating your time?

Schedule Everything:

Would you be willing to put all the key elements of this plan into blocks of time in your schedule?

Would you be willing to time block all your primary tasks, responsibilities and interruptions, so that you can balance everything in your schedule?

Project Managers:

Why do projects fail?

Project managers love to make plans and build perfect project timelines. Projects **almost always** fail because the plan never gets into the schedule of the people who are supposed to do the work.

When will you start asking the 'when' question?

11

11 Reality

The reality of when

Does your time look like this?

9 **Meet with Joe**   Start times,
                        but no end times.

10

11   Lots of empty
                        spaces to fill with
12   interruptions.

1 **The big presentation**

2

3   **Endless to-do list**

           File report

4   Check email

           Update expenses

5

           Tons of things to do,
           some on a list but most in your head
           and no idea "when" you will do them.

I have too much to do!

Sequential time:

When we try to remember what we have to do in our head or even make a to-do list it is always a sequence of tasks. We can only represent a sequence using our mammalian or emotional brain. We talk to ourselves about having too much to do because we can never **see** an entire sequence of tasks in our head. We feel guilty because that is what the emotional brain is designed to do.

When will you do this?

A visual relationship with time

Or does your time look like this?

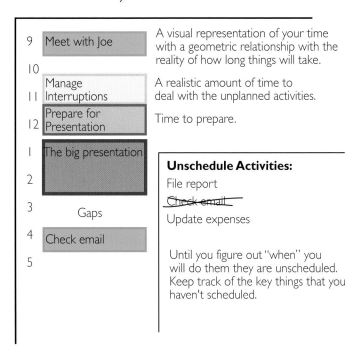

9 Meet with Joe	A visual representation of your time with a geometric relationship with the reality of how long things will take.
10	
11 Manage Interruptions	A realistic amount of time to deal with the unplanned activities.
12 Prepare for Presentation	Time to prepare.
1 The big presentation	
2	**Unschedule Activities:**
3 Gaps	File report
	~~Check email~~
4 Check email	Update expenses
5	Until you figure out "when" you will do them they are unscheduled. Keep track of the key things that you haven't scheduled.

Visual time: *Blocks of time in your schedule*

A time block forces us to make a visual representation of our time. This lets us access the advanced spatial reasoning capabilities designed into the positive visual area of our brain. As we dynamically adjust our blocks of time, we *PLAY* with the future in which we have complete control over the reality of our time.

11 Reality

A new dynamic relationship with your schedule

There was a time when you said "I am going to be one of those organized people." You bought the best leather day planner or gadget and you organized the perfect day.

Then life happened. The reality of the volume of things you have to do and your weak relationship with interruptions set in. Your perfect day was ruined and you realized that you would never be one of those organized people.

This old relationship with your schedule no longer serves you. Given the new reality of work, producing results at an unprecedented level will require an entirely new **dynamic** relationship with your schedule:

The more you **put** in your schedule,

the more you **look** at your schedule,

the more you **move** things around in your schedule,

the more you will have this new **dynamic relationship** with your schedule.

Don't worry about doing everything exactly when you said you would do it. Look in your schedule and honor your original intention when you put the item in there.

what if you don't do this?

Consequences

What would the consequences be if this doesn't happen?

What will happen if this doesn't go as planned?

What will be the consequences for **you** if you don't keep your promise?

What will be the fallout for others or for the project if you don't keep this promise?

What else might happen if you don't take this on?

Unspoken Question: Have you thought through the consequences of what will happen if this doesn't go as planned sufficiently, such that you are called into action?

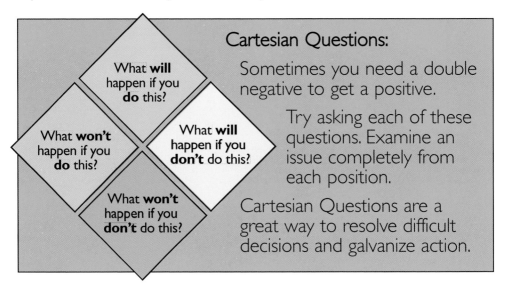

What **will** happen if you **do** this?

What **won't** happen if you **do** this?

What **will** happen if you **don't** do this?

What **won't** happen if you **don't** do this?

Cartesian Questions:

Sometimes you need a double negative to get a positive.

Try asking each of these questions. Examine an issue completely from each position.

Cartesian Questions are a great way to resolve difficult decisions and galvanize action.

Impact

Team:

Could you be responsible for the impact on the whole team if this doesn't go as planned?

> What other projects or activities won't happen if we don't do this?

> What other plans could be affected if this doesn't happen?

What are the consequences for the team if this doesn't go as planned?

> How could this affect people outside the team?

> Who else could be affected?

> How will this affect our level of trust?

Unspoken Question: Are you absolutely committed to do what it takes to handle this?

Exit: Is there a new level of ***resolve*** to stay in action and be unstoppable?

Let's consider what might happen if this doesn't go as planned.

12

The Ratio of Motivation

90% Carrot   10% Stick

The point of Question 12 is not to create fear or guilt.

The point is to first build a solid foundation of positive visual motivation by sufficiently answering the first eleven questions. The balancing act is to explore what could go wrong just enough to **galvanize** commitment and action.

Action requires a 3 sided box:

You push against your promise. You are hemmed in by the impact and consequences. You have no choice but to get into action and move toward what you want.

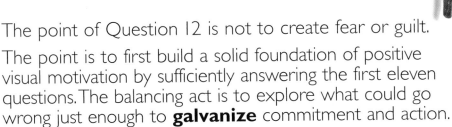

p
r
o
m impact
i ● *action* →
s consequences
e

vision for
what you
want

---

is that a promise?

Is that a promise?

Have you fully considered how you will do this, how you will stay on track and when you will do it, so that you can make a promise with 100% certainty?

Are you willing to promise this?

Yes or no?

Do I accept your promise?

For the question asker:

Before you accept their promise, ask yourself,

Am I 100% certain that this person will keep this promise?

Are there conditions I need to add before I accept this promise?

Am I willing to accept this promise?

Am I willing to support this person to keep their promise and be successful?

Unspoken Question: Are you clear on the cost of making weak promises?

Is that a promise?

Team:

Have we as a team fully considered how we will do this and how we will stay on track? Have we scheduled the details so that each of us can individually make a promise with 100% certainty?

Are we, as a team, willing to fully accept this promise and fully hold each other to account?

Exit: Is the promise real? Were Questions 10, 11 and 12 fully explored before the promise was made?

If you want someone to win, support them to keep their promise, before they make it.

The BS-O-Meter:

You are equipped with a highly sensitive BS-O-Meter. Being polite, we pretend not to notice when the readings are going off the chart. **STOP** pretending not to notice. Using your BS-O-Meter serves you and the people with whom you work.

beep!
beep!
beep!

13

How to create a strong promise.

When is the **best** time to negotiate a promise?

> **Before** you make a promise, **while** you are promising, or **after** you have made a promise?

After you make a promise you have limited power to renegotiate.

Learn to catch yourself before you say "yes."

Saying no or responding with a counter-offer may not be acceptable in the culture of your team or organization. However, you can always raise concerns or add conditions before you say yes.

> I am curious,
>
> ## Is this request non-negotiable?

So let me be clear. You are promising that nothing will get in the way of you keeping this promise. No client emergencies, no excuses, no reasons will stop you.

And, if there is anything that could get in the way of you keeping this promise, you will communicate it to me within 48 hours.

Yes.

{...long pause...}

Yes.

I accept your promise.

14

can
I count
on
you?

Can I count on you?

Can I count on you to keep this promise?

Is there anything else you will need from me?

Can I count on you to complete this without any further follow up from me?

Are you really going to complete that in the next (30) days?

Is there anything from the past we need to resolve about not keeping any promises to:

me?   the team?   yourself?

Is there anything you need to do or say to address any promises you haven't kept in the past?

Can we re-establish trust such that I can count on you to keep your word?

WARNING:
This conversation is not nice.

What will it take to produce results at the highest level?

Straight Conversations.

You may have a pattern for being nice or avoiding conflict. This pattern will not serve you here. Business transformation cannot happen without accountability. Accountability requires difficult conversations.

Advanced Accountability:
The point is not to keep your promises.

You could keep all your promises and still lose the game. Your job is to ask for what you want. Your job is to design a big breakthrough and make promises that you don't know how to keep. Advanced accountability is the art of stretching yourself.

Your job is to play full out, stay on track, manage your focus and stay in communication when you realize you are off track or stopping yourself.

Your job is to engage in rigorous accountability conversations and honor the essence of your original intention even when it doesn't go exactly as planned.

14

Your job is to fail hard and often, learn what you need to learn and dive into what's next with no loss of energy or enthusiasm.

---

14 Accountability

Can we count on each other?

 Team   Would each of us be willing to play with 100% accountability for the entire project?

Can I count on you to complete this without any follow up from me?

Have we resolved any promises that were previously broken?

What will be the reporting structure?

How will we stay in communication?

How quickly will we communicate if there is a breakdown or anything else standing in the way of us keeping our promises?

Unspoken Question: When have you not kept your promises in the past?

Objection: You don't trust me.

Response: I am willing to trust you 100%, if you are willing to trust yourself. Are you willing to trust yourself and play at 100%?

Exit: Is there a new relationship with integrity? Is there a new level of ownership?

What is the difference between **your** accountability and **our** accountability?

Personal blame blocks effective communication.

Accountability is a two way street. It takes two people to make a promise. When you accept a promise, **you** are also making a promise to support the other person to be successful.

Just as the CEO is accountable for the total results of the company, the CEO is also accountable for all the promises in the company.

If you want more accountability in your organization, start with yourself. Stand for and be accountable for the entire success of the organization. The more you stand for, the more others will join you in your stand.

We begin by standing for the accountability of our entire team.

"Do we as a team have a sufficient level of **relationship, communication** and **accountability** to keep our promises to each other?"

14

Bring back the stick

Having a 'stick' conversation is critical to business transformation. It serves people to be held to account for their promises.

> Are you strong or weak with accountability conversations?

> Do you know how and when to use the stick conversation appropriately?

> Do you establish and maintain relationship before having accountability conversations?

Practice the stick conversation:

> (**Always** re-establish relationship first)

> > I request that... (x)

> > It is completely unacceptable that... (y)

> > > Can I count on you to keep your promise?

> > > Are you the right person for this project?

> (Finish with)

> ...and I am completely committed to your success.

Exercise:

Have one 'stick' conversation per day for the next week

where
was
the
breakdown?

Where was the breakdown?

Why do people hide problems? We hide problems because we can't, in the moment, see a solution. We hide problems to buy time to figure a way out. We want to look good, be the hero and find a solution on our own.

Individually, we have a limited ability to solve problems on our own.

It is difficult to ask powerful questions or engage in an inquiry by yourself. It is akin to cutting your own hair. It is possible to cut your own hair, but not recommended.

Your job is to ask the questions that will allow the people you support to see a solution. With the right question, problems are always easy to solve. We find the right question by engaging in the inquiry and asking lots of questions. The **greater** the number of people committed to finding a solution and engaged in the inquiry, the **faster** the problem will be solved and the higher the quality of the solution.

As with all of the accountability questions, Question 15 is potentially dangerous. Asking this question in order to find someone to blame is the quick path to shutting down team communication. The more you ask this question with authentic curiosity and a commitment to team excellence, the more you will create an environment of inquiry.

Where was the breakdown?

Where was the breakdown?

> What specifically went wrong?
>
> What could you do better next time?
>
> Where was the breakdown in communication, tracking or reporting?
>
> Where else did a breakdown occur?

Team: 𝌆

> What were the hidden assumptions?
>
>> What was the breakdown behind the breakdown?
>
> How can we prevent this from happening again?
>
> **Objection:** I'm not to blame.
>
> **Response:** Everyone is responsible in part. How do you think we can prevent this in the future?
>
> **Unspoken Question:** How did you hide or ignore the breakdown?
>
> **Exit:** Is there a new space of inquiry around what went wrong? Is curiosity present?

Real power is the ability to confront a breakdown with no loss of energy.

15

Where is the plan weak?

Focus your questions on where the plan is weak and any other sources of worry, stress or concern.

> Where do you have the least amount of confidence in your plan?

Always move toward fear.

The questions, by their nature, will move people toward fear. Fear is a conversation about what we don't want with a set of associated emotions and body responses.

At a higher level, fear is the lack of a vision for what we want and a plan to get there. Focus your questions on doubt, worry, fear and any hesitation or lack of action. Ask the questions required to turn fear into a plan for success and then schedule the required actions.

Get in action.

The questions will generate business transformation. Business transformation will quickly disappear if it is not put into action. Always create a promise, schedule the required actions and set up an accountability conversation.

Fear is a lack of action.
Always schedule the next action.
Action cements business transformation.

16

what did you learn?

What did you learn?

The question **'What did you learn?'** transforms failure into growth, problem into opportunity and conflict into challenge.

Without this question you can only feel regret and blame yourself or others for past mistakes. With this question life becomes a process of growth and each pitfall a gem of discovery.

Acknowledgement drives growth.

One of my executive clients was wired for success. He was focused on the elusive next milestone in his career. However, after interviewing and working with his team, I noticed a distinctive pattern. The harder he drove his team the more they would withdraw.

The homework was simple. At the end of each project cycle, he would schedule a short "What did you learn?" conversation with each team member. He would ask them the questions, **acknowledge** whatever results they had achieved and thank them for their hard work. It took about 90 days for the shift to settle in. What emerged was a vibrantly productive team.

What did you learn?

How did this project go?

Did we achieve the result?

What worked?

What accomplishments make you proud?

What didn't work?

What would you do better next time?

Where did you stop playing full out?

What did you learn?

What was most important?

How will what you learned make a difference in the future?

For what would you like to be acknowledged?

How did you grow?

What were the surprises?

How will this be useful in the future?

Is there anything else you would like to say to fully resolve the completion of this project?

Unspoken Question: Are you willing to learn and grow from this?

16

16 Development

What did we learn from this process?

Team:

> Where were we **on** our game?
>
> Where were we **off** our game?
>
> Where did we develop a new level of...　teamwork?
> > communication?
> > organization?
>
> What could we have done better?
> > What areas of performance need improvement for the next project?
> >
> > What new systems do we need to put in place?

What did we learn?

> What new capabilities did we develop?
> > At what new level will we be able to work next time?
> >
> > **Exit:** Is learning present?

What would a true learning organization look like?

At all ages, the human mind is a learning machine. **Humans can not, not learn.**

What if everyone in your organization was a master at business transformation and having 17 Questions conversations?

What is the future of business?

What would your organization look like if **Business *Transformed*** was business as usual? Consider that this is what business as usual will look like in the next 18 years.

At the present rate of accelerating change in the world today, a workforce that can dynamically adapt and drive business transformation will be the basic requirement for competitiveness.

What will long term impact be if your team is not willing to ask the questions required for real growth and leadership?

16

6 advanced principles for asking the questions:

1 **Don't speak after you ask the question:** The 5-20 seconds of silence is where all the work happens.

2 **Check for a shift before moving on:** Has the current question had an impact? Are the exit conditions met?

3 **Strengthen the weakest link:** Go back and strengthen the weakest areas of the conversation.

4 **Don't ask the Unspoken Question:** Be patient, they will get there on their own, or somewhere even better.

5 **Get curious about where they are weak:** A breakthrough in the weakest area will create a breakthrough in all other areas.

6 **Always move toward fear:**

What are 1 or 2 things that are worrying you right now?

Where do you have the least amount of confidence?

Final exit test:

Has fear been replaced by confidence?

17

what's

next?

What's next?

What's next?

Having completed this, what are you considering for the future?

What else do you want to take on?

Having completed this, what else is now possible?

What do you want next?

Team: Is this project complete?

Did we produce the result?

What is the follow up?

What now needs to be tracked or managed?

What next steps would take what we have accomplished to a new level?

What's next?

What's next?

Was this useful?

Was this conversation effective?

Did we keep our contract for this conversation?

Is this conversation complete?

Is there anything missing?

Are any of the conversations weak?

Can we recap and debrief the key points of this conversation?

What were the specific promises and when will the actions take place?

When is our next meeting?

What is our next follow up structure?

Is there anything you want to say to complete this conversation?

Unspoken question: Are you willing to play at an even higher level?

Exit: Is there an experience of renewal?

17

17 Questions in 45 Seconds

You can have a business transformation conversation that will transform an entire company in 45 seconds:

1 Ask yourself, "Which question is missing?"

2 Let your intuition guide you to the missing question.

3 Ask that question.

When you look at the successful transformation of a business, you can always trace the process back to a single defining question from which everything shifted. Sometimes it can take hundreds of questions and weeks or months to find that question. Other times you will know exactly what is missing and ask that question first.

What comes next?

Have a 17 Questions conversations in:

45 seconds   45 minutes

or a series of conversations over 45 days

A business transformation conversation doesn't have to be formal. There are many ways to have this conversation. Remember the first question is simply "How are you?" Ask this question everywhere. With a little practice you will naturally flow into business transformation conversations.

The business transformation learning stages;

1   **Read the book:** Read it again. Read it aloud.

2   **Immerse yourself:** Get this book into your life. Keep it in your pocket. Cut this book open and put your favorite pages up everywhere.

3   **Practice:** Practice asking the questions. Read them aloud. Be a beginner.

4   **Schedule conversations:** Schedule 45 minutes with a friend or associate to have a business transformation conversation.

5   **Get more support:** Get a buddy. Find a 17 Questions power-user. Visit www.BusinessTransformed.com.

6   **Create a 17 Questions relationship:** Schedule regular conversations over a 45 day period.

7   **Create your Business *Transformed* community:** Give the book to everyone on your team. Schedule discussions about business transformation.

8   **Play with the questions:** Make them your own.

9   **Keep asking the 17 Questions:** Everywhere. All the time. They will pop out of your mouth.

10 **Master the Business *Transformed* conversation:** Mastery is the ability to keep inquiring into the questions.

Business*Transformed* Programs

Business*Transformed* I-Day Breakthrough Series:

Business*Transformed* Engage: This I-day program provides mastery of Questions I to 9 and offers a profound shift in business, life and work.

Productivity*Transformed*: This program delivers a breakthrough in focus and peace of mind through mastery of Questions 10 and 11. It also delivers a powerful new relationship with email, meetings and interruptions.

Business*Transformed* Certainty: In business, accountability is confidence. Mastering Questions 12 to 17 provides certainty in every interaction and a foundation for accomplishment.

The I-day Breakthrough Series is offered live for the public in major cities, online as a web-based teleclass or on-site for corporations. Programs include follow-up coaching to ensure success.

Business*Transformed* One-on-One Coaching:

Silver Series Breakthrough Program: Work with a certified Business*Transformed* coach to achieve your breakthrough. Working with a Business*Transformed* coach is also a great way to master the 17 Questions from the inside out.

Platinum Executive Breakthrough Program: What will it take to achieve breakthrough results? Selected individuals are invited to work directly with Paul Gossen to transform their business, work and life.

Business*Transformed* *Manager as Coach* Training:

Team Thinking: This 4-day program gives managers and team-leaders the capability to inspire teams into top performance.

The Art & Science of Coaching: This 16-day program, accredited by the **International Coach Federation**, has been established as a leading corporate coach training program worldwide.

Take action today. **Visit: www.BusinessTransformed.com**